DEDICATION

This book takes you on a journey into the minds of women and how they think.

I dedicate this book to all the men out there trying to understand the female mind.

I've spent over half a decade searching for these answers, so I hope you find everything you've been searching for...

www.ingramcontent.com/pod-product-compliance
Lightning Source LLC
Chambersburg PA
CBHW062031290426
44109CB00026B/2589
9780646719214